A PLACE TO PAY
ATTENTION

BONNIE THURSTON

INDEPENDENT INNOVATIVE INTERNATIONAL

Published by Cinnamon Press
Meirion House,
Glan yr afon,
Tanygrisiau
Blaenau Ffestiniog,
Gwynedd, LL41 3SU
www.cinnamonpress.com
The right of Bonnie Thurston to be identified as author of this
work has been asserted by her in accordance with the Copyright,
Designs and Patent Act, 1988. Copyright © 2014 Bonnie Thurston
ISBN: 978-1-909077-39-3

British Library Cataloguing in Publication Data. A CIP record for
this book can be obtained from the British Library.

Designed and typeset in Palatino by Cinnamon Press
Cover from original artwork 'New River Gorge Bridge' ©
dreamstime.com
Cover design by Jan Fortune

Printed in Poland

Cinnamon Press is represented in the UK by Inpress Ltd
www.inpressbooks.co.uk and in Wales by the Welsh Books
Council www.cllc.org.uk

Acknowledgments & Thanksgivings

Several of these poems have appeared previously. They include "The Last Farm" *Anglican Theological Review* (88/2, 2006), "Carbon Footprint" *The Christian Century* (126/18, Sept. 8, 2009), "Southern West Virginia, Summer, 1996" (*Hints and Glimpses*, Three Peaks Press, 2004), "How to Cross the Mountains" *Monkscript*: Literature, Arts & Spirituality (1, 2002), "My Darkness Bright" *Spiritus* (9/1, 2009). I am grateful to the editors for permission to use the poems here and especially to the editor of Three Peaks Press, Michael Woodward, who published my first two collections of verse. "West Virginia Ghost Town" won 3rd place in the long poem category of the 2013 West Virginia Writers, Inc. competition.

I am eternally grateful to the English teachers in the public school system in Raleigh County, WV (1958-1970) and the English faculty at Bethany College, Bethany, WV (1970-1974) who taught me to love and encouraged me to write poetry. Heartfelt thanks to Ruth Bidgood, Anne Cluysenaar, Stevie & James Coutts, Cheryl & Marc Harshman, Charl & David Kappel, Jane Rotch, Esther de Waal, Michael Woodward and the Society of the Sacred Cross, Tymawr Convent, Monmouth, Wales and the Cistercians of Our Lady of the Angels, Crozet, VA, USA. These friends (and several un-named others) care about poetry and supported and encouraged this poet who would otherwise have put down her pen.

Finally, my profound gratitude to Cinnamon Press for publishing this collection and especially to editor Jan Fortune for her courage, hospitality, many kindnesses---not to mention her patience with me. Her own considerable literary gifts enhance her considerate editing which is done with such care and gentleness.

Contents

For Ruth Bidgood

An 'offering/of forgotten things'
With affection and gratitude

> *There is the life*
> *and telling of the life.*
> *There is completing*
> *and forgetting,*
> *and the offering*
> *of forgotten things.*

From Ruth Bidgood's poem 'What Then?'
from the sequence 'Land' in her book *Symbols of Plenty*

A Place to Pay Attention

Southern West Virginia, Summer, 1996

The misty, Appalachians
are our mother.
They smother, embrace,
make of us isolated,
independent people,
reclusive as red foxes.

No clarity of earth or air,
here it's noon before
the fog burns off
and the haze hangs
in the hollows
all day long.

Nestled in her breasts
the sky seems narrow.
When the moon
comes over the mountain,
it hangs in her cleavage,
an exotic jewel.

Rutted, meandering roads
follow streams and rivers
reddened by the mines.
Company towns
are peeling off the hills.
Tipples totter crazily,
erector sets gone mad.
The squeal of the wheels
is silenced, rails rusted,
and almost nobody goes
down to the coal face
for honey in the rock.

...

But this land is home to me,
sweet as a whippoorwill song
when dewy evening spreads out
like a familiar, faded quilt.
Being here makes my heart
sing like yellow sunflowers
by an unpainted shed.

From Here

The pattern of mountains and valleys
rolls out like the ridges
of an ancient washboard.
Dark blue-green mountains alternate
with light yellow-green valleys,
both veined with snaky, narrow roads,
dappled by blindingly incandescent tin roofs.

The lay of this land is God's joke,
all crumpled up to make us stumble
as we race toward the smoky horizon,
carefully unfolded in soul harrowing splendor
and so emblazoned on the heart
that no matter how high we rise, or far we go,
no place else can ever be home.

My daddy's people came from here,
and whether I claim my patrimony
or try to be someone I am not,
the life blood of these mountains is my own,
courses through the twisted strands
of my green and rocky life
like a storm swollen stream.

The Over Mountain Men,
Sycamore Shoals, 1780

They gathered from mountain farms up the hollers,
homesteads in long, rolling valleys.
Sinewy men with long rifles, untrimmed beards,
their raggedy families in tow,
came from log cabins with mud
in the chinks and for the floor,
fireplaces from great, rough stones,
men who, when they saw smoke
from another's chimney, moved on.
What they had didn't look like much
to lose, but it was theirs.
Some fool English officer
threatened to march in a foreign army,
take back hard won homes.

It don't do to threaten mountain people,
and these had faced worse than the army
of an idiot king from across the sea:
weather and beasts, serpents and pestilence,
the ire of the first mountaineers
from whom they wrested the land.
What was a blustering red coated lord
in knee britches and silver shoe buckles?
They meant to kill him, and they did.

Hundreds of them gathered here
where the Watauga could be forded
and the shoals sang of freedom.
Some of them stayed to guard
the women and the young.
The rest marched over the mountain
to do the work of war.
The women waited; the river sang,
and directly the men folk returned,
gathered up their grateful kin,
went silently home to mountain farms.

12

Stand by Sycamore Shoals on the Watauga,
behind the rebuilt stockade, the historical markers.
Old folks stroll with their sticks of an evening.
A Cherokee woman and a white woman
walk with a little child between them.
Picnickers eat food they didn't sweat for.
Listen. You can still hear the shoals sing:
free and strong, free and strong.

Legacy of the Dutchman's Pipe

Some folks seek flashy rewards:
big cars, big cigars, big jewels,
huge gadgety houses,
stocks galore, money in the bank.

I have a taste for life's
quieter compensations
because as a young woman
I was shown how to hunt
Dutchman's Pipe in the woods.

It's common enough,
but seldom seen
because the vine is green
and blooms high up.
Most folks can't see
the flower for the tree.

Finding that wildflower
instilled a permanent preference
for what can be seen
by looking up
or looking differently
at what's right here.

Pigeon Top Mountain

Early spring, the best time
to be on the mountain:
undergrowth not thick,
but wild flowers awake
brilliant yellow, subtle blue;
trees leafing yellow-green,
white dogwood, redbud spindles.
Scat suggests mammals aren't,
but snakes are still asleep
or too winter torpid to care.

Early spring, the best time
to listen to the mountain,
to the gentle rustle
(like breath in placid sleep),
listen for the next word
from the voice whispering
just at sound's threshold,
Don't struggle.
You can't be farther on
than where you are.

Personal Geography

We are marked
by the place we call home,
not the house or people
(though that is true, too),
but by the land.

I am the daughter
of the mother of mountains,
child of the earth's oldest river,
suckled by Appalachian breasts,
sung to sleep by New River's roar.

The road ended, petered out,
at the top of the mountain
where we lived.
Without noise or street lights
we could hear and see.

Have you heard
a whippoorwill at dusk,
or heard
the conversation of squirrels,
or the wind with the trees?

Have you seen ribbons of mist
hanging on the hills,
waiting for the sun to kiss away
fog's diaphanous drapery
and bring the day to birth?

What, I ask you,
is so lovely
as a patch of trillium
in a stand of oak,
a rhododendron thicket in June;

what so fearsome
as a Copperhead
coiled in leaves,
a black bear with her cubs
met unexpectedly in the woods?

In mountains that held black
diamonds of enormous cost
to the good people who dug them,
I have seen these things
and others too wonderful to tell.

My home was rugged, isolating,
astonishing in its beauty.
It left me with rough edges,
an undeniable earthiness,
a taste for solitude.

I was formed
by a land so grand
that it broke the boundaries
between me and mountains
clean open

and still calls me
to soar like a hawk
above the narrowness of self,
to rise on the wind
and sing and sing and sing.

How to Cross the Mountains

Pack your car the night before.
Study the map for back roads.
Sleep well; leave early.

Stop at the gas station
where the Negro lady
at the counter
will make you
a country ham sandwich
on white bread
with yellow mustard.
While you wait,
smell the coffee,
eves drop on the farmers.

Drive up the valley
between blue hills.
Don't be blinded
by sun on tin roofs
of square, wooden houses,
bright as the blue eye of God.
Notice the feathery outline
of conifers,
pink apple blossoms,
lacy as a pair
of old bloomers.
At some point turn west,
start up the mountain.

Regress four weeks.
Trees aren't leafed out,
but there is a field
of wild purple iris,
a cloud of yellow butterflies,
a pretty white church
in a forgotten village.

Play the radio. Loudly.
Turn it off and sing.
Pass a lumber truck.
Let a motorcycle pass you.
At the top of the mountain,
in the shadow of a rock,
look out across hills
stretched out like paper cuts outs,
old as the Potter's hands.
Say grace. Eat lunch.
Wipe yellow mustard
off your chin.

Wave salutations
to sheep grazing
in mountain meadows.
Don't speed
down the mountain.
It's more dangerous
than it looks.

Resist the urge to make time
by cutting over to the highway
because crossing mountains
is about the journey itself.
There is a horizon
beyond the horizon,
even more to see
than the profusion of wonders
right before your eyes.

Summer Solstice

Weather at solstice
is unsettled, stormy.
This June's roared by
wild, wet and windy.
Yesterday streams
raced high and muddy.
Today they subside,
resume normal channels.
But where the road curls
around Short Creek
the Great Gray Heron
has not returned,
a reminder, perhaps,
that the balance
hasn't quite righted,
like the stream's,
its inner reality,
while clearing,
is not yet limpid.

Choosing Gifts

I would like to take
dear far flung friends
who have been so kind
gifts from a home
as if I had one,
gifts from a heart land
so deeply planted
in me that my blood
blossoms red with it
and every poem
is rooted there.

But how does even
gratitude compress
in music or word
or hand made thing
autumn morning mists
rising to reveal
the mountains' secrets,
or the birds' singing,
circling upward
toward the God of hearth
and homelessness?

Not Sinai

I cross again
into the valley of Virginia.
In the north, trees
are heavy with apples.
Afton Mountain's
familiar fog is filleted
by a thin blade of light
reminiscent of the knife
that forty years ago
dissected my heart,
first given and broken here,
eventually mended,
offered to the God
of serrated experience.

I was not Moses.
This was not Sinai.
There was no night
pillar of fire, only night.
Cloud did not lead,
but obscured
almost everything,
settled stubborn as mists
that delay hazy dawn
around the still, beloved
Blue Ridge Mountains.
I pulled up stakes,
folded my tent,
journeyed on.

The Last Farm

I have driven by it for years
on the way to the city,
watched the siege as suburbia
steadily encroached on,
battered away at
the last farm.

But this spring morning
I was not prepared
to see the black indentation
where the barn had stood,
each Christmas sheltering
a cut-out crèche.

Now all that remains
as I cross the line
from rural to urban
is the shadow
of something once there,
the precarious balance
between here and gone
irrevocably and forever tipped.

Emptying the Family Home

They lived here forty years.
It has taken us three
to empty the family home.
Now we are at the end.
The house is an empty shell,
the yoke of joy and sorrow gone,
the detritus of four lives
carried out in black plastic bags.
We marvel at what our parents kept.

Separated by seven years
my brother and I
grow closer in the process
of remembering and renouncing.
There is so much to cling to,
so much to cast away.
Each of us accepts ownership,
makes peace with loss,
offers absolution.

The realtor comes, looks,
lists the property.
We are decisively cut adrift
from the past's moorings,
forced to look ahead instead of back.
Like Abram to gain the promise,
we leave country, kindred, father's house.
Now we make our own home place.
Now we must be present where we are.

Passing Through

Passing through fertile farms in Ohio
on a crystalline spring day,
I think of home, mountains, sibling.
Flat fields undulate slightly
an optical illusion from harrowing,
thousands of parallel lines of stubble
as if God ran the divine comb
through an improbably blonde crew cut.

So much limpid azure air,
alive with layers of sea-side clouds,
so different from our home place
where sky was a blue gray triangle
peeking furtively through mountains.
This much sky makes me nervous,
far too much exposure
to heaven's unpredictability.

My brother moves frequently,
owns multiple modern houses.
For twenty years I have lived
in shabby sameness, tucked
between hills on a serpentine road,
love my stone gorged garden,
the growth of things I've planted
now deep rooted as I am.

I pass solid, rectangular houses,
widely spaced and lonesome looking,
miles of black, loamy, ungreened fields,
an old well populated cemetery,
granite markers pointing accusing fingers,
am content to be traveling briefly
across this sun lit plain
toward the rough places of home.

Conveyors

I come home late by the back road
ruined and resurfaced by coal
which took the modest mountain homes
to install immense conveyors
to roll the stuff to the river
where barges carry it away.
The long belts slither through our hills,
their lights like malevolent pearls
strung to strangle friendly darkness.
Tonight the moon is nearly full,
draped mysteriously in mist,
eclipsed by the shining serpent.
Like Cleopatra's little asp
they strike the breast of the mountains,
bring some relief and others death.

A Place to Pay Attention

It isn't much of a place.
You would pass by and not notice.
But it is the well spring
of my insight and delight.
No estrangement of over-familiarity,
I live on this anonymous patch
amid arresting seasonal surprises.

The upper garden, for example,
is now apparently a love nest.
Behind rows of beets and runner beans
the earth is churned up,
a jumble of green and brown clods.
I remember it is rutting season,
the deer in their frenzy of desire.

Like so many small things,
green, battered earth reminds me
to harmonize, tune my soul
to a world where love making and life
were intended to be the norm.
How would I know this
without a place to pay attention?

Fire Flies

Balmy June evening,
air soft on the skin,
the moon rising,
Venus hangs on the horizon.
Verdant, mysterious
points of incandescence
move randomly, languidly
in the semi-darkness.

It is not yet full night,
but it will come.
Because I know this,
I am doubly grateful
in this still twilight
for a child's delight
that the world is studded
with graceful, glowing things.

Surprise

With eyes to see,
ears to hear
there are still surprises
in well known places —
like turning a corner
on a familiar path,
encountering eye-to-eye
a Great Gray Heron
preening in the sun,
or noticing at pond's edge
a turtle eating a fish head,
nibbling down the delicacy
of its spinal column,
then seeing the flash,
hearing the splash
as that fish's kin
leaps up to devour
an iridescent dragon fly
for whom this day held
a terrible surprise.

The Eyes Have It

An unseasonably warm day,
a March wind stirs
winter slime of a pond
suddenly alive with eyes
emerging from murky obscurity:
bullfrogs' bulbous and looking
permanently thyroid impaired;
on phallic, sinewy necks
the scaly, reptilian visage
of multiple box turtles.

Facing the weirdness of water
full of floating eyes
I think of Gloucester's vile jelly,
Donne's threaded eye-beams,
the inscrutable eye of God
pyramided in old paper money.
I know an original darkness
shadows all our seeing,
but in this peculiar moment
there is only sight.

Toad

I unearthed one
the exact color of the soil
I'd troweled planting salvia,
lifted it to tilted stone
on which it looked to be
a lump of warty earth.
It was absolutely motionless,
not even the slightest
bellows of breath.
Was it wounded?

I hadn't the courage
to touch or turn it,
see unintended disemboweling.
Better to leave unmolested
this small embodied dignity,
its unblinking stillness,
refusal of panicked motion,
its silent, stoic waiting
for what would happen next,
its fate in my soiled hands.

Tempters

Walking a graveled road
one warm May morning,
rhododendron in full bloom,
air fragrant with new grass,
I stumbled upon it.

It was startlingly pretty,
but so small
I nearly missed it,
only six inches long
and thinner than a pencil.

Platinum brown,
copper patches ringed
with silver bands,
a Copperhead's beauty
is deceptive, deadly.

A snake in the grass.
What other dangers hide
in serene spring meadows?
What tempters beckon
without pitchfork or horns?

Snake Skin

A very long, slightly crumpled
tube of mottled, gray cellophane
laced in autumnal stubble
beside a country road.
At first, I think it litter,
then experience adrenalin charged
shudder of recognition.

What constriction,
what great itch for the future
causes a creature
to crawl right out
of its comfortable, old skin?
What pain and pushing
forwards that process?

I walk nervously on hoping
to avoid the former occupant —
not for the size of the snake,
but the size of the questions
its shed skin raises
like a cobra from a basket
I thought long ago closed.

Wild Turkey

Oafish, ill proportioned,
he strutted by the garden
feathers a glory
of bronze iridescence.

Clearing underbrush,
I found him nestled
in the roots of a tree,
body the color of earth.

Unmoving, unblinking,
I left him undisturbed,
thought he came to die,
felt oddly honored.

For days he reposed
inertly vulnerable
to predators, to me,
then was gone, leaving

six speckled shells
neatly broken open
where she had roosted
for dear life.

Of Impossible Design

Two braved human danger,
picked their way down
to full bird feeders.
The rest of the wild turkeys
lumbered across the upper hill,
impossibly shaped lumps
with tiny legs, neck, heads,
but dressed in feathers
of golden, byzantine beauty.

We, too, are of impossible design,
but dressed in divine light.
Some of us glimpse it,
struggle in spite of dangers,
to make our way to seed
the word sows on many soils.

Hawk

At daybreak, through fog
just visible on the chapel's cupola
a raptor surveys his diocese.
Later in the day
floating on a current of air
in the limpid summer sky,
he surveys his possibilities,
eyes and talons sharp
for an unsuspecting groundling.

I am too large for his lunch.
Still, I walk as if trying to escape
today's ominous reminder
of rapacious caprice,
life's unpredictability.
Who knows what larger eye
and sharper claw
lurks behind this hawk
in the blue infinity of air?

Good Mountain Folks

Serpentine country road
in the late afternoon,
it was not a safe place
to try to block the way.
But the scruffy young man
in faded shirt and jeans
had stopped his old pick up
in order to protect
an immense box turtle:
as big as a sauce pan,
crawling across the road
speed of cold molasses.
If looks tell truth he was
not the sensitive type,
but the boy had been taught,
as good mountain folks are,
to respect his elders.

The turtle barely moved.
Not a car came along,
but we both knew one could,
so the young man bent down,
holding it at arm's length
because old guys can snap
off the random finger,
carried it carefully
across the narrow road
and put it down safely
deep in the weedy berm.
We never spoke, but smiled
through a parting thumbs up,
young man and old woman,
strangers on a back road.
What ever you are told,
this is who mountain folks are.

All These Awakenings

Brightening March collides
with winter temperatures.
In early, bright dawns
even heavy frost, light snow
seems full of promise.

Somewhere spring's first snake
stirs in the brittle skin
it will soon leave behind.
A sleepy mammal stretches
and licks its lusterless fur.

Distant as fleeting memory,
the song of a summer bird
echoes through bare trees,
causes vernal vibrations
in my hibernating heart.

All these awakenings
are glorious mysteries.
I stop counting winter beads,
turn again toward the light
at the core of all my longing.

Unseasonable Joy

On this mundane mountain
March is always mercurial.
The day between lashing rain,
a storm of sleet and snow,
I pull on green rubber boots,
squelch up the cleft in the hills
toward a blue triangle of sky.

A mossy, branched thing
protrudes from the stream bed.
I pull at sucking mud
releasing a great, full rack,
still attached to its skull,
complexity of bone knit to spine
intact, intricate as Belgian lace.

After happiness with many does
like the four shaggy –coated ones
my wet walk startled,
this buck died of old age.
Perhaps this accounts
for my unseasonable joy,
the mute pleasure of wonder.

My Darkness Bright

I am a woman 'of an age,'
no longer sleep soundly
but inhabit darkness as well as day.
I awaken periodically
to monitor the movement of stars,
take night's temperature,
offer the parched, sleeping world
the water of murmured prayer.

So I am conversant with moons:
the icy howl of the Wolf Moon,
hushed blooming of the Grass Moon,
Harvest Moon, ripe and red as apples.

By my trysting moon,
moon of my restless heart,
is the blue-white natal silence
of the Long Night Moon
whose distant, maternal face
smiles on her frozen world,
makes winter night luminescent
and my darkness bright.

Singing Up the Corn

The people native to this land
planted their crops at night,
singing to the seeds.
They called it 'singing up the corn,'
knew that dropping seed
by moonlight into mother earth
was joining the moist eternity
of becoming and growth,
joining a song in progress.

When I have weeded my garden
and sit quietly among the plants
waiting on warm, rich earth
still vaguely redolent of manure,
I feel the energy of their growing,
the faint cosmic vibration
humming the instinctual fruitfulness
that animates the universe
joining a song in progress.

West Virginia Ghost Town

It proved not to be
a good idea,
the impulse to take
in the too small car
my aging parents
back to the coal camp
where my father worked,
where 'company store,'
were the magic words
for all things dreamed of.
There was practically
nothing left of it
but the beautiful
stone foundation work
done by Italian
immigrant craftsmen:
no company store,
ranks of small houses,
each identical,
none owned by dweller,
marching away from
the working heart hub,
the mine head, tipple,
machine shop, bath house
where as a filthy
child I was once bathed
to the male horror
of my father's mates.
(He feared mother's tongue
more than masculine
mute disapproval.)
It had all vanished:
the Methodist Church,
the soft ball diamond,
the colliery band
long ago silenced,
the life of the place
evaporated.

Even the stinking
environmental
nightmare, the gob pile,
had burned itself out,
its residual
red dog no longer
useful for firming
muddy mountain roads.
The bright autumn day
seemed somehow darker.
We should not have come,
and went home silent
as the place we left.
Living memory
would have been better
than this holocaust
of a peopled past.

Precious Rocks

...I will give a white stone, and on the white stone is written
a new name that no one knows except the one who receives it.

(Revelation 2:17)

Perhaps this is why
I have always been
a collector of stones,
lined dusty window sills
of home, retreat house,
vacation cabin
with small impediments
of meandering journeys:

a tiny, purple chip
from Sinai's height;
Wyoming soapstone
smeared with copper ore;
deceptively flecked schist
full of fool's gold;
once, in Virginia,
where rock is red
with ferrous oxide,
a three inch obelisk
of gray granite
fused to milky quartz;
Iona's green marble,
the crimson pebbles
of its martyr's beach;
(my perennial favorite)
a water worn smooth
white palm sized stone.

The hand luggage
of my travels
is heavy with them,
the basement littered
with boxes of petrified souvenirs
from forgotten places.

Reader, do not chuckle
in bemused indulgence.
'Stony the road I trod.'
On life's rocky road
it is serious business
to search the hard,
animate beauty of stone
for one's own hidden
and secret name.

New River

It has an umbery glow
in the full moon,
like satin ribbon
on a faded wedding dress,
like ancient brush painting
a la chinoiserie.
It is immensely old,
older than the mountains
it has composed,
through which it thunders
in brisk *allegro.*
Respecting its wildness,
I would not ride its rapids.
You do not tame
mountain makers.
I have moved away,
seen other landscapes,
learned other languages,
but never forgotten
mother-river, heart
of the world it made,
always glowing,
moon lit in memory.

Disconnect

In is our state's sesquicentennial.
We have settled down
to an orgy of history and nostalgia,
of memory and wishful thinking.
We re-imbibe cultural divides
east and west of the Alleghenies,
re-attend secession conventions,
rehearse Lincoln's legal dilemmas.
Wearing fake Victorian attire,
we attend balls and speeches.

Meanwhile, all over town
they are cutting down trees:
ancient oaks along U.S. 40
our first national highway,
the enormous maples
fronting the primary school,
ornamentals sheared and stunted
by the old Episcopal church.
Even my kind neighbor
is lopping down his lovely trees.

Distracted by remembering,
no one makes a fuss
about murdering memory,
killing connection to a past
now buried deep in rings
that will no longer
ripple out in time.
I hear the trees weeping,
lamenting a loss
lifetimes will not replace.

Holding Too Tightly

Autumnal morning
and I can't let go
of what used to be:
how we drove to town
and saw them sitting
on their wonky porch,
she in a print dress,
he in overalls.

Their house is long gone,
though always for me
palpable absence
when I wind this way
through shadowy wood
following a road
which follows a creek,
cause of the house here.

Two mammoth oak stumps,
sentinel headstones,
now guard the escape
from time's tyranny.
Like flies in amber,
dry stone wall restrains
the liberation
of memory's slippage.

Memory

I am cooking rhubarb,
stirring the stringy
green glory of it.
The smell takes me straight
to Great Uncle Mark's farm
where Grandma grew up,
her generation gathered;
the terror of being sent
early, small and alone
to the hen house
to steal breakfast eggs
from huge, terrifying birds;
awed laughter of Great Aunts
telling and re-telling the tale
of how their Granny hung
by the neck until dead
the cat that ate the chicks
warming by the stove;
boy cousins in the barn
hunting black snakes;
the men smoking
or chewing and spitting
off the flagstone porch
from which the long row
of rhubarb trailed off
toward the back pasture
and into this memory.

Grandmother Muses on Fire

The stove gave the only light.
The only sounds were the hiss
of a bit of wet wood,
the creak of her rocker
on uneven floor boards.
Never take fire for granted,
she counseled,
and watch out for progress.
Long ago, across the ocean
when night was coming on,
women smoored the fire,
buried it in ashes,
laid down peats
with powerful prayers.
Before morning they'd lift them,
the mother's breath
fanning coals to life,
to the first, flickering flames.
Those hearth fires never died.
They banked them real good.
When children left to marry,
they took home fire with them,
like a living memory,
the life breath of family.
Bonding fires they're called.
They say at the Clearances
the clans brought their fires
with them on the ships
and across the Alleghenies
to our old, green mountains.
I wonder about that, but
I heard tell of one bonding fire
kept for three hundred years,
last by an old man all alone.
Then a dam burst
and flooded his valley,
covered his hearth
with 200 feet of water,

smothered his fire, killed
the connection to his kin.
It was mighty sad, she said,
staring into her own fire
and the watery conflagration
of that poor old man's past.

Widow's Sweater

Six degrees yesterday
with fine snow in the air,
sparkly, like bits
shaved from a diamond.
I lit a fire in the stove
laid with wood I'd split
from trees up the hill
felled in summer storm,
wore a fuzzy, old sweater
knit from left over yarn,
oh, maybe twenty years,
another lifetime ago.
Fusty with wood smoke,
this morning I hung it
outside to air,
forgot it until the dark
was pricked by stars,
bright, distant cousins
of those flakes of snow.
I fetched it in,
heavy with the cold,
draped it over a chair
where, all evening
it gave off chill,
perfumed my bedroom
with the sharp smell
of winter night,
the faint memory of fire.

The Old Ways

I married late;
my husband died early.
We had no children.
Now that I am gray
I worry about the old ways.

To whom will they
pass when I pass on —
how to walk quiet in the woods,
how to know false
from true Solomon's seal,
how to predict first frost
or help a garden grow?
Who'll care to quilt, knit,
make good corn bread
or Sassafras tea
from pungent, pink roots?
Who will sing
from the shape of the notes
or know 'Shady Grove,'
who recognize the Sight
as good but eerie gift?

Every single one of us
links past and future.
Every culture is fragile
as a grandmother's
china tea cups.

Salvation

Granny Ellis down the way
was a hard shell Southern Baptist
and a good neighbor for that.
She felt responsible for the souls
all along our side of the road.
Every spring, after Easter,
when rhubarb was thick and red,
she'd cut a mess of it,
fill a brown paper poke,
one for each household,
commence her itinerant ministry.
She'd knock on every door,
ask the occupant, *are you saved?*
holding out the offering of rhubarb
which still tastes to me like salvation.

Driving to Chapel Hill

Sunday after Sunday I drive
to the same rural church,
know where the road
can't be trusted,
where creeks rise
after summer storms,
where ice patches in winter,
and heedless deer cross
at dawn and gloaming.
I know where the heron fishes,
when wild turkeys roost,
the parade of seasons,
the costume of particular trees,
anticipate the ridge top
where I can see for miles
the bosomy swelling of hills,
the cleavage of field and valley
heaving up to meet the sky
which, in dropping
every sort of weather,
can strike or caress.
I know the rooted serenity
of a small, white chapel
with amazing windows
which has stood its ground
for more than a century
at a now-forgotten crossroad.
I know with gratitude
the blessing of invitation,
the mystery of entering
the inmost life
of a place and a people.

Palm Sunday Driving Westward

I see in the greening
but not leafed out world
why the Scots-Irish
settled and loved
these rolling hills
so like the land they left,
gnarled outline of trees
like home's horizon.

I see the flattened place
the old wagon track ran.
Usually hidden by forest,
it is the mystery of the road
not taken, or even known,
stark, tangled image
of the absence of expectation
an alternative might exist.

We settle in places
and for what seems familiar.
Today's procession proclaims
the way does not take us
where we thought to go.
The road itself changes,
remade in the shadow
of three twisted trees.

Sublunary Shadow

With washed feet,
having supped,
I leave liturgy
in the country church
full of heaviness,
weighted
with wondering.

I ponder what
we are passing
over into on this,
the darkest night
of last meals,
bloody sweat,
betrayals.

An oddly horizontal
slice of half moon
is veiled by clouds.
On the ridge
a solitary farmer
plows his field
in sublunary shadow.

Arrived, Departed, Returned

Easter was framed by birds:
flash of kingfisher
angling in Short Creek
as I drove to the Vigil,
impossibly thin gray heron
glimpsed in rising mist
in route to Sunrise Service,
symbolic birds sinking into,
rising from the waters,
drawing down the night,
presaging the light,
recalling the dove
if not the Voice which
commissioned the Beloved
for passion now past,
flowering now manifest
in lily, dogwood, trillium
which, like the birds,
decorate death's demise,
celebrate life's champion
arrived, departed, returned.

Poised for Foliage

Rain formed a silver patina
on wet, black branches
poised for foliage.

With no hint of leaves
pink flowers erupt from limbs
of an apricot tree.

A plowed furrow undulates
with uncovered life:
insect, earthworm.

A field is full
of small, yellow explosions:
cowslips, primroses.

Spring's tiny mysteries
psalm the primacy of surprise,
the precariousness of joy.

And somewhere deep within
my own sap rises
wet with the fire of life.

Old Farmer at the Foot of the Cross

Brother, you were treed
like a coon by a pack
of blood hungry hounds,
flung up against
the darkened sky,
nailed like a fresh hide
to dry on the barn.
So how is it I see
'round your thorny head
a glow like kerosene light?
Some folks say
you mark the way
through woods
and waters home.
Well, buddy, I reckon
I'm ready to go.

El-Shaddai

I am a mountain woman.
What I know is this:
every hill
to which I lift up my eyes
is Mount Sinai —
fiery in autumn,
stern in winter,
resurrective in spring,
filled with green life
under summer's thick cloud.

To those with ears to hear,
in every season
mountains are alive
with the mystery
of the still, small
voice of God
thunderous with love
for trembling us,
whispering in the hollows,
thou, thou, thou.

In the Church Yard

(Hebrews 11:3)

In faint, westering light
I think, not incongruously,
of the Hubble telescope,
of the just arriving
still steady glow
from long dead stars
enlightening eternity's field,
these luminous dead:

the Elder, a water witch who
saved many a farm;
the pastor's wife who
 quietly made things right;
the simple Deacon who
lived for Sunday's service;
the beloved only son whose
kind heart stopped at twenty.

There are hundreds more
planted on this hill,
lights in their generation
and in the present darkness
denizens of the eternal,
unhidden city, pillars of fire
and grace given signposts
on life's last, inevitable journey.

Taps

This perfect autumn day
with its wood smoked air
is pure Americana,
a page from Norman Rockwell:
the white clapboard church
with its tiny steeple and bell,
the basement hall tables
with the meal laid out,
the ladies hovering.
The line of mourners
wearing ill fitting black suits,
stiff collars and ties,
dark somber patterned dresses,
hands clasped or elbows linked,
snakes through the manicured church yard
with head stones bearing their own names,
down to the neighbor-dug grave
where the V.F.W. Memorial Team
(men older than the deceased)
waits to shoot their guns,
to fold and present Old Glory,
to thank the grieving widow
for her man's service
to his grateful country,
to play 'Taps' for the dying
of this, our way of life.

Well Water

Endowed with sacred
character, wells span
three cosmic orders:
water, earth and air.
Their water is held
by earth, then given
to creatures of air.

Well water bubbles
from hidden places.
It comes from within
the bosom of earth
as one element
offers its essence,
its self, to the rest.

Quiescent and clear,
the living water
settles deep within,
awaiting its time
of rising to light,
of being consumed,
giving life for life.

Twilight

I watch the light retreat
up the hill behind the house
past the vegetable patch,
past the pear tree, the apple.
It reaches the edge of the woods
where a doe, illuminated, golden
nibbles low leaves
of something flowering white.

Every creature drawing breath
has deep hungers
that cannot be satiated
by all the delectable possibilities
in this good, green world,
malnourished places
poignant as transitory light
going up on the ridge.

Preparations

It is hunting season,
but deer are out in force.
Coats roughening for winter,
they gorge in growing darkness,
gobble acorns as the last
oak leaves blow away
in wind gone arctic.

I prepare for long winters,
store canned goods,
stack stove wood,
hope the mind's furnishings
are sturdy enough
to sustain in darkness
until the great greening.

Shooting Star

It was an otherwise gruesome journey
begun in pre-dawn darkness,
bidding adieu to a beloved place,
people I have come to love,
hurrying to cross mountains
ahead of violent winter storm,
traversing a nasty bit of highway.

But above traffic, tractor trailers,
just as the horizon glowed golden,
I saw the not seen since childhood
when my father took just me
to the beach long after bed time
to sit beside him safely, silently
watching — a shooting star.

Country Roads Take Us Home

There is nothing much
hot or hurried about
our shaded lanes.
Ours is not a place
of super highways,
but twisted back roads,
lane and a half at best,
a place that teaches
the necessity of yielding,
the grace of giving way,
in part by narrowness,
in part by the obscurity
of noon green darkness
in forested valleys
and hair pin turns
hiding what comes next.
We cussed coal trucks,
but now there is
sad lonesomeness
in the winding emptiness,
the legacy of pot holes,
brokenness they left behind.
Still, travelling here
reveals the harsh beauty
of sparsely populated places,
the proud integrity
of folks who stay on
knowing that somehow
origin is destination,
that the road makes us
what we become,
and, however circuitously,
will take us home.

Going Home

Going up the long, loved valley
between mauve mountains
a flock of migrating birds ascends
in an undulating cloud,
but I miss their message.
Light, silver on the illuminated side
of winter black trees,
moves across the mountains
like the suggestion of a smile.

It is a long journey.
I am often tired.
But when the moon is a smudge of light
rising behind broken clouds,
brilliant stars appear above the ridge,
I, too, swim in ebony darkness,
awash with gratitude
that I do not need to know
the pattern or end of my orbit.

Carbon Footprint

Mine is reasonably small
having always lived low,
turned off lights and faucets,
eschewed useless stuff,
reused, recycled.
I do not aspire to shrink it,
but, like the first people
in these green hills,
I want to leave
no footprint at all,
to move through life
in gentle, charitable silence
not disturbing fragile things,
cosmic balances
or the universal pulse
so that, when my candle
sputters into darkness,
the tiniest leaf is unmoved
by the wisp of its rising smoke.

Notes on the Text

Most of the poems in this collection are set in my 'home place,' the southern Appalachian mountains of the U.S.A. (The 'lach' in Appalachian rhymes with 'catch.' When people say it the other way, we know they aren't from here and probably don't know much about us.) The lyrics are arranged in a gently narrative manner, and several are themselves narratives. Places and languages have regional dialects and metaphors or 'sayings' with localized meanings.   You will only hear the faintest echo of our dialect in this volume. (Ethno-linguists say in some places it echoes Elizabethan English.) There are several phrases that have specialized connotations here that may be unknown elsewhere, and some references that might be unfamiliar or unrecognized outside our region. I hope these brief notes provide helpful information. Mostly I hope they aren't necessary and that the poems stand (or fall!) on their own.

'Southern West Virginia, Summer, 1996': A 'tipple' is a coal processing plant.

'My Darkness Bright': Native Americans named the moons of the year in connection with events in the cycle of the seasons.

'New River': The tourist industry takes visitors to run the rapids on this dangerous river of which most locals are wary. The photograph on the cover of this book is of the New River Gorge Bridge.

'Precious Rocks': 'Stony the road I trod' paraphrases a line from the hymn 'Lift Every Voice and Sing' words by James Weldon Johnson and music by J. Rosamond Johnson.

'The Old Ways': 'The Sight' is an uncanny ability to see the future (and things other people don't see) which seems to 'run in families,' often those with origins in the Scottish Highlands.

'In the Church Yard': A 'water witch' is a person who can find subterranean water with a forked stick.

'Taps': The V.F.W. is the Veterans of Foreign Wars,   an organization for military veterans.

'Twilight': 'Going up the ridge' is an Appalachian euphemism for death.

'Shooting Star': 'Tractor trailers' are enormous, double length lorries.